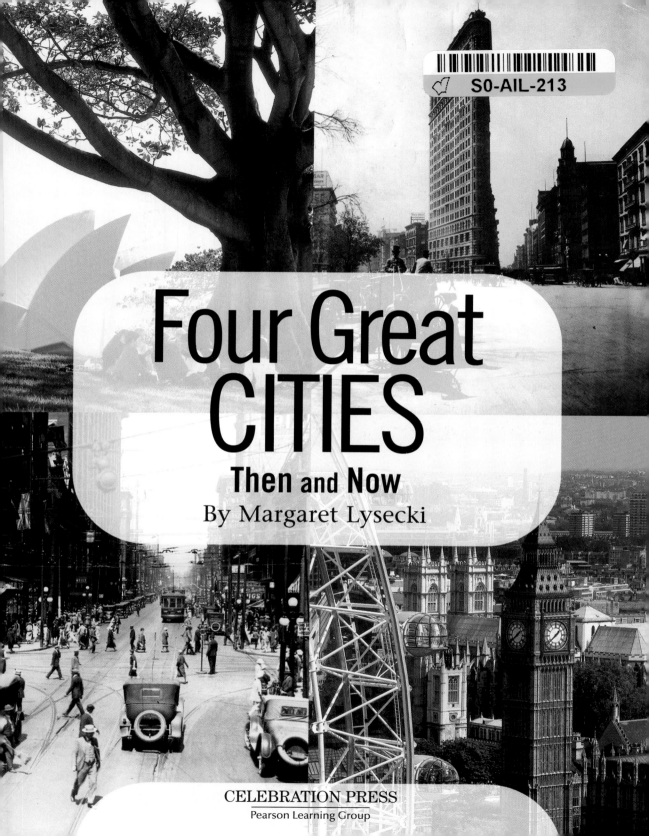

Four Great CITIES

Then and Now

By Margaret Lysecki

CELEBRATION PRESS
Pearson Learning Group

The following people from **Pearson Learning Group**
have contributed to the development of this product:

Joan Mazzeo, Dorothea Fox **Design** | **Editorial** Leslie Feierstone Barna, Cindy Kane
Christine Fleming **Marketing** | **Publishing Operations** Jennifer Van Der Heide
Production Laura Benford-Sullivan
Content Area Consultant Dr. Linda Greenow

The following people from **DK** have
contributed to the development of this product:

Art Director Rachael Foster

Martin Wilson **Managing Art Editor** | **Managing Editor** Marie Greenwood
Kath Northam **Design** | **Editorial** Jennie Morris
Helen McFarland **Picture Research** | **Production** Gordana Simakovic
Richard Czapnik, Andy Smith **Cover Design** | **DTP** David McDonald

Dorling Kindersley would like to thank: Shirley Cachia and Rose Horridge in the DK Picture Library; Ed Merritt in DK Cartography; Johnny Pau for additional cover design work; and Mariana Sonnenberg for additional picture research.

Picture Credits: Alamy Images: Dominic Burke 9b; Don Jon Red 7tl; Felix Stensson 23tr. Corbis: 11tl; David Ball 24–25; Bettmann 5bc, 9t, 10; Hulton-Deutsch Collection 4br, 20ca; Scott Houston 15br; Hurewitz Creative 17; Louis K. Meisel Gallery 16cr; Schenectady Museum; Hall of Electrical History Foundation 5tcr, 14b; Paul A. Souders 27br; Underwood & Underwood 1tr, 1bl, 2, 4tr, 22; Ron Watts 20–21; Chad Weckler 12–13; The Brett Weston Archive 16b; Michael S. Yamashita 13t. DK Images: Mitchell Library, State Library of New South Wales 28tl. Mary Evans Picture Library: 8, 15bl. Getty Images: Hulton Archive /Fox Photos 27bl, 28b. Masterfile UK: Rommel 23cbr. National Library of Australia: 26. Photolibrary.com: 6–7, 23cbl. Reuters: Andrew Wallace 21b. Getty Images: Paul Souders 25tr; Space Frontiers /Taxi 45,c. Jacket: Hulton Archive/Getty Images: front bl. Masterfile UK: Lloyd Sutton front t.

All other images: DK Dorling Kindersley © 2005. For further information see www.dkimages.com

ISBN: 0-7652-5240-6

Color reproduction by Colourscan, Singapore
Printed in the United States of America
6 7 8 9 10   08 07

1-800-321-3106
www.pearsonlearning.com

Contents

A Changing World

During the twentieth century, the world's population grew from fewer than 2 billion to more than 6 billion. In 1900, almost all of the world's population lived in rural areas. By the year 2000, more than half of all people lived in urban areas, or cities.

Over the years, the great movement of people into cities has presented many challenges. People in cities now have an increased demand for food, housing, clothing, goods, and employment. Transportation is often difficult as well, because so many people have to get from one place to another. Also, because many city dwellers come from many different places, they have to learn how to interact with people from other cultures. All cities face the problem of meeting such needs. However, people in cities have done a remarkable job, working together to overcome these challenges.

On the following pages, you will read about four cities: London, New York, Toronto, and Sydney. You will discover how these cities have changed over the past hundred years and how each city has become a great **metropolis**.

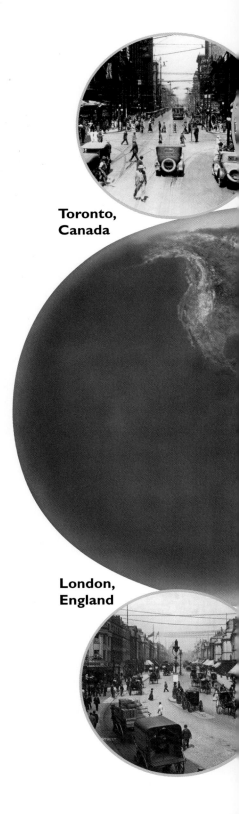

Toronto, Canada

London, England

New York,
United States

Sydney,
Australia

London
Ancient Port to Modern City

About 2,000 years ago, the city of London was a Roman port on the Thames River. By the 1900s, London was a huge city. Its port had become a busy place where goods were **imported** and **exported**. London had many successful workshops, factories, and businesses. Attracted by job opportunities, people moved to London in great numbers. London's built-up area soon spilled over into the surrounding countryside. In 1900, this vast **metropolitan area**, known as Greater London, had a population of 6 million and covered an area of 620 square miles.

By the end of the twentieth century, Greater London's port area continued to thrive as a center for importing and exporting goods. As planes, trains, and trucks became faster and more efficient, they brought in goods from all over the world. By 2001, the population of Greater London reached almost 7.2 million.

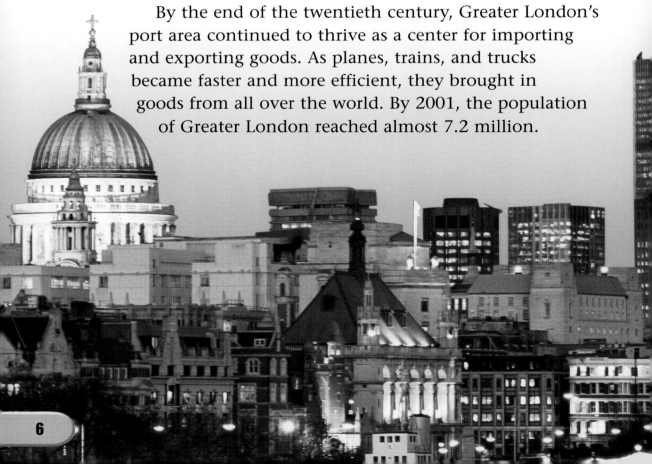

Some of London's Asian **immigrants** settled near Brick Lane Market (above).

Londoners

In the early 1800s, most people in England lived in the country. However, by 1900, more than three-quarters of the population lived in cities or towns. About one-fifth of these people lived in London and the surrounding areas. Many people came from rural areas to work in the city. Others came from overseas.

People from Ireland flocked to London during the Great Potato Famine that lasted from 1845 to 1849. Large numbers of Jewish people arrived in the late 1800s. After World War II, thousands **emigrated** from the West Indies, Asia, Africa, and the Middle East. These new Londoners changed the character of the city. As a result, London is now an exciting, **multicultural** city.

Industry

In the mid-1800s, London became wealthy through trade with countries all over the world. People found work at the docks, loading goods for export and unloading imported goods. Some people found work in **manufacturing**, banking, or medicine.

Many workers lived in rows of inexpensive houses, built closely together in order to provide shelter for as many people as possible. As more people moved in, some of these areas became **slums**. New homes were later built away from the city. When public transportation became available, many people moved to these new suburban areas and commuted to the city.

The docks on the Thames River bustled with activity in the early twentieth century.

Children play in a London slum.

As time passed, factories moved outside London. The companies that remained in the city managed the shipping of English goods around the world. Foreign banks moved their offices to London. A large insurance industry began to develop as well.

Between the 1960s and the 1980s, the port of London declined. At the same time, England's manufacturing industry declined, leaving many unemployed. However, with London's large population and growing number of tourists, the city still needed many workers in service industries, especially in transportation, health care, and entertainment. Today, London is one of the world's most important **financial** centers, a headquarters for global banking. It is also the capital of the United Kingdom and the center of English government.

In the 1980s, part of London's docks was transformed into a stylish media and finance center, now known as the Docklands.

Transportation

London streets in 1900 looked very different from those same streets today. Back then, they bustled with pedestrians and **omnibuses**. Cars were rarely seen. To avoid the crowded streets, people used "steamers," or steam-powered ships, to travel on the Thames River. These steamers provided another efficient method of transportation.

People also traveled through London by rail. Railway trains carried commuters to their places of employment in the city. In 1863, the world's first underground railway system opened in London. The London Underground, sometimes called "the Tube," allowed passengers to avoid traffic on the busy streets by traveling through underground tunnels.

This 1902 photo shows omnibuses, streetcars, and pedestrians crossing Westminster Bridge.

Horse-drawn cab, 1884

Black cab, today

Today, many forms of transportation are used throughout London. The streets are crowded with heavy automobile traffic. Many residents and tourists travel on London's famous red double-decker (two-story) buses or in black taxicabs. Railways continue to serve thousands of daily commuters. The London Underground now has more than 270 stations.

London's location also makes it a hub for air travel between Europe and North America. The city has five airports to serve world travelers. Its largest airport, Heathrow, is one of the world's busiest. More than 64 million passengers pass through it each year.

London remains fascinating and exciting because it is both historic and modern. The Tower of London, nearly 1,000 years old, shares the city with the London Eye, the world's largest observation wheel, which opened in 2000. Between them, these two London landmarks cover centuries of English history.

Thousands of double-decker buses travel around London.

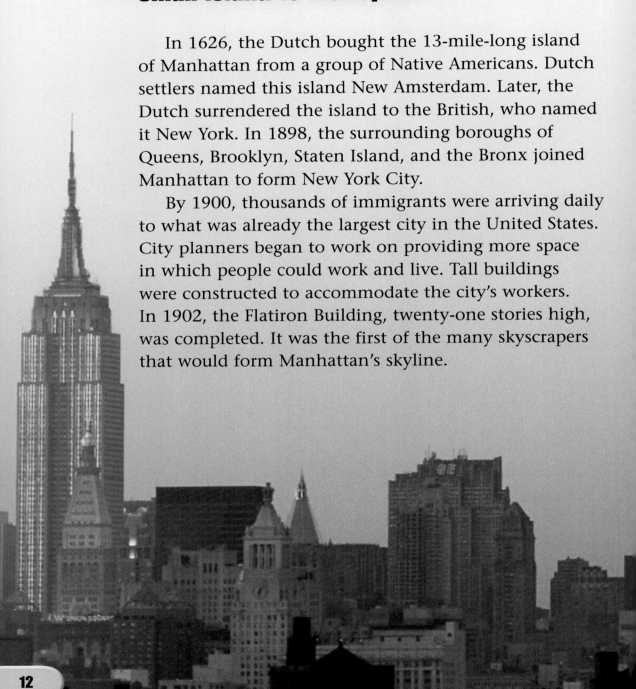

New York
Small Island to Metropolis

In 1626, the Dutch bought the 13-mile-long island of Manhattan from a group of Native Americans. Dutch settlers named this island New Amsterdam. Later, the Dutch surrendered the island to the British, who named it New York. In 1898, the surrounding boroughs of Queens, Brooklyn, Staten Island, and the Bronx joined Manhattan to form New York City.

By 1900, thousands of immigrants were arriving daily to what was already the largest city in the United States. City planners began to work on providing more space in which people could work and live. Tall buildings were constructed to accommodate the city's workers. In 1902, the Flatiron Building, twenty-one stories high, was completed. It was the first of the many skyscrapers that would form Manhattan's skyline.

New Yorkers

By 1900, millions of people had immigrated to the United States, seeking the chance for a better life. The first stop for many immigrants who entered the country was New York. A large number stayed, helping to make New York a diverse, multicultural city. At that time, more than half of New York's working population had been born in another country.

Harlem has a large African American population.

Over the years, thousands of African Americans moved from southern states and settled in New York. Many lived in Harlem, a neighborhood in northern Manhattan that became a center of African American literature, art, dance, and music. Today, African Americans make up 25 percent of New York's population.

Today's New Yorkers are proud of their city. The cultural mix makes it an exciting, **cosmopolitan** place. Visitors and native New Yorkers alike can hear a variety of languages, taste foods from around the world, and enjoy many cultural experiences.

Industry

In the 1900s, New York was the headquarters for U.S. industry. More vessels passed through its port than through any other. Many factories were built near the port in order to ship goods overseas.

People became interested in the arts, and the entertainment industry thrived. Broadway, a street that runs the length of Manhattan, became home to many theaters. The term *Broadway* is now linked with the best of American plays and musicals.

Broadway is the center of New York's theater district.

This photo shows Broadway in the early twentieth century.

Today, as the site of many banks and global financial institutions, New York is a leader in world business and finance. At the city's famous **stock exchanges**, stocks and bonds are bought and sold, or traded daily. New York is a cultural center as well. Many people look to New York to identify new trends in music, art, fashion, and literature. Manhattan's garment district, where clothing is made, continues to employ thousands of people. New York is also a major media center where many books, magazines, and newspapers are published. Radio and television stations and many top advertising agencies are based in the city. Because millions of tourists visit New York each year, many people are also employed in hotels, restaurants, galleries, and museums.

Then and Now

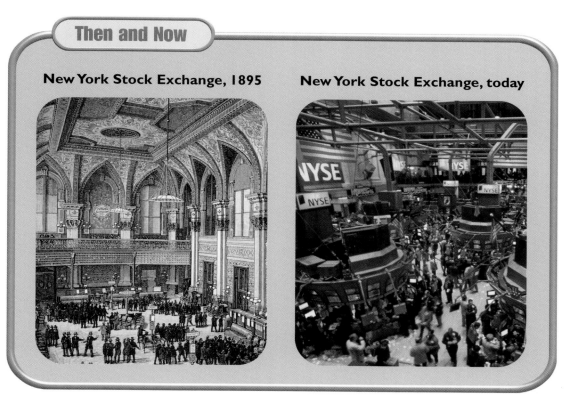

New York Stock Exchange, 1895

New York Stock Exchange, today

Transportation

In the early twentieth century, New York's large population made transportation a challenge. Horse-drawn carriages were crammed, and the streets were overcrowded. Planners built an elevated railway, known as the "El," but its noise frightened horses, and cinders and soot fell onto the streets.

Because of these problems, city planners decided to build underground. In 1904, the first 9 miles of tracks for the subway, an underground railway, were completed. Today, New York has more than 700 miles of subway tracks and 450 stations. More than 3.5 million people travel on the subway every day.

Before the subway (above), the "El," or elevated train, took New Yorkers around the city.

New York's yellow taxicabs prepare
for another busy day.

Above ground, motor vehicles eventually replaced horses and electric-powered streetcars. New roads and bridges were built so people could drive around the vast city more easily. Today, there are sixty-five bridges and several tunnels linking the city's five boroughs. Ferries also carry commuters and tourists from one borough to another. The city's famous yellow taxicabs, which first appeared in 1907, can be seen on almost every corner. The honking of their horns is a hallmark of the hustle and bustle of city life.

New Yorkers know that the "Big Apple," as their city is nicknamed, has a lot to offer. With its diverse population, tall skyscrapers, vibrant cultural offerings, and thriving financial district, New York is one of the world's greatest cities.

Toronto
"Meeting Place" to Thriving City

Toronto is located on Lake Ontario, one of the five Great Lakes in North America. Originally a French trading post, the area was a settlement occupied by the British in the late 1700s. The British named the city *Toronto* (a Native American word that means "meeting place") in 1834.

Like London and New York, Toronto grew in size as people came in search of a better life. By 1900, it had railways, factories, and a port. In 1904, however, a fire destroyed more than a hundred buildings. Out of these ruins, a new city developed. Skyscrapers were built, and Toronto's present skyline began to take shape.

In 1998, Toronto and the five communities surrounding it merged to form one city. The city and its neighboring areas cover 243 square miles. Today, Toronto is home to almost 5 million people.

Torontonians

Most of Toronto's early immigrants were British. After World War II, large numbers of immigrants from other countries arrived. They were encouraged to be loyal to their new land but also to preserve their culture—an idea known as "the Canadian mosaic." A mosaic is a picture or design made with many small pieces. Each piece has its own shape and color, but is also part of a larger picture. As home to more than eighty **ethnic** groups and more than one hundred languages, Toronto is a big part of the Canadian mosaic.

Toronto's Chinatown has one of North America's largest Asian populations.

Although there are some distinct communities, such as Little Italy, Greektown, Little India, and Chinatown, there are also neighborhoods in which many different cultures live together. Today, the fastest-growing immigrant groups are from Asian countries. These new Canadians have contributed much to the culture, art, education, and industrial development of the city.

Lumber mills in northern Ontario helped Toronto become the city it is today.

Industry

From its beginnings as a center for fur trading, Toronto has been an ideal location for business and trade. The opening of the Erie Canal and the building of railways led to rapid growth in industry. Lumber mills and tanneries, places where animal hides are made into leather, were built. Toward the end of the nineteenth century, commercial farming was expanding and lumber was used to build cities and towns.

The discovery of gold, silver, and other valuable minerals in northern Ontario had a big impact on Toronto. It helped the city develop as a center for planning, financing, and directing mining developments. Much of Toronto's mining helped supply industries in the United States.

Hydroelectricity is generated by the powerful waterfalls of Niagara Falls. Electricity is produced and supplied to many industries.

The 1900s saw the growth of new industries. Electrical equipment, chemicals, cars, aluminum, pulp and paper, radios, home appliances, and aircraft were all manufactured in Toronto. Many of these industries relied on cheap hydroelectric power supplied by Niagara Falls, located 69 miles from the city.

Today, Toronto provides one-sixth of all jobs for Canadians. It is Canada's banking capital and the home of the Toronto Stock Exchange. Just as New York is to the United States, Toronto is the printing and publishing center of English-speaking Canada.

Recently, many films and television shows have been made in Toronto, earning it the title, "Hollywood North." Toronto is also known for its food and beverage production, technology, and pharmaceutical, or medicine, manufacturing.

Toronto is a popular location for moviemaking, and the city stages a film festival every year.

Automobiles and electric streetcars carried passengers along Yonge Street.

Transportation

At the beginning of the twentieth century, Torontonians traveled from place to place by omnibus, electric streetcar, or car. When the streets were covered with snow, people rode in horse-drawn sleighs. The city was also growing in importance as a railway center. In the mid-1900s, Toronto and its surrounding areas became the first places to use a computer-controlled traffic system.

Today, Toronto's highways wind in all directions. The city's modern transit system includes streetcar, bus, and subway routes. This system connects residents and visitors with shopping centers, sporting and cultural events, and the downtown core. Commuter trains and buses bring people into the city from surrounding areas. Almost one-quarter of city workers use public transit, but many prefer to drive. As in many large cities, traffic jams are frequent, and solving this problem is an ongoing challenge for city planners.

Toronto's road network is very large.

Then and Now

Toronto streetcar, 1908

Toronto streetcar, today

Despite its many challenges, this city by the water retains a small-town friendliness. It's a place in which people of various cultures and backgrounds come together to create the Canadian mosaic.

Sydney
Convict Settlement to Olympic City

In 1770, Captain James Cook claimed the entire east coast of Australia for Britain, naming it New South Wales. Later, the British government decided that New South Wales would be an ideal place to establish a **penal** colony. In 1788, a fleet of ships carrying more than 1,000 people—most of them convicts—landed in Sydney Cove.

The convicts became Sydney's workforce. By the early 1800s, some of them had been pardoned and given land to farm. In 1851, the discovery of gold in New South Wales attracted thousands of people to the area. In the years that followed, Sydney prospered. Advances in transportation were made and the city's harbor flourished. Almost 150 years later, Sydney was awarded the honor of hosting the 2000 Summer Olympic Games.

Sydneysiders

Sydney is home to the largest urban population of Australian **Aboriginal peoples**. Aboriginal peoples have lived in Australia for more than 50,000 years. The Eora people, Aboriginal Australians, were the first Sydneysiders. Much of the Aboriginal culture was destroyed when Europeans arrived in Australia. Today, however, Aboriginal Australians again proudly celebrate their culture through storytelling, dance, and art.

Traditional Aboriginal culture is popular today with both tourists and Australians.

Many groups have contributed to Sydney's multicultural face. For more than 150 years, Sydney's culture was influenced by European immigrants, particularly those from Britain. After World War II, many immigrants came to Sydney from European countries such as Greece and Italy. In more recent times, people from Asian countries have contributed to Sydney's multicultural neighborhoods, celebrations, and restaurants.

Industry

The land around Sydney is rich in minerals and metals. Mining was responsible for much of Sydney's early growth. The gold rush in the 1850s brought great wealth, as well as more British and Irish immigrants, to the city. About the same time, coal mining grew dramatically with the discovery of rich new mines. Coal mining had begun in Australia in the 1790s, but production increased after these discoveries. By 1900, coal was being mined not far from Sydney in places such as Lithgow, Newcastle, and the Illawarra district.

The gold rush of the 1850s was the first of many in Australia. These prospectors from the 1880s are shown outside their hut.

Australia Day activities on Sydney Harbour attract visitors from far and wide.

Today, manufacturing is as important to Sydney's industry as mining. Sydney's factories produce everything from clothing to electronics. A large percentage of the nation's products are exported from Sydney's harbor.

Sydney is also one of Australia's most popular tourist destinations, attracting 4 million visitors annually. Sydney is the headquarters for Australia's main financial institutions and is a thriving center for business and the arts. In addition, Sydney and nearby areas in New South Wales are home to a number of research centers specializing in medical, agricultural, and aquatic study.

Then and Now

Sydney surfers, 1931

Bondi Beach, today

Transportation

As early as 1850, Sydney planners knew that the city would have transportation problems unless a bridge could be constructed to connect the North Shore to the city center south of the harbor. Construction of the Sydney Harbour Bridge began in 1926, and the bridge was officially opened eight years later. Today, more than 150,000 vehicles cross the bridge daily, while large ships pass easily beneath it. The Sydney Harbour Tunnel, built in 1992, offers an alternative way to travel from the north to the south of the city.

It took eight years to build Sydney Harbour Bridge.

SYDNEY BRIDGE CELEBRATIONS BE THERE!
MARCH 19ᵗʰ 1932

Once it was complete, the Sydney Harbour Bridge revolutionized transportation across the city.

Driving in the city can be a challenge. The road network is confusing, and traffic is often congested. Fortunately, Sydney has a well-developed public transportation system. A rail network with double-decker carriages moves people to and from the central business district. A **monorail** runs along a scenic route through Sydney to Darling Harbour. It is mostly used by sightseers.

For more than a century, ferries have also been a practical method of transport across the harbor. Day or night, they can be seen crossing the water. They carry Sydneysiders to their jobs and bring tourists to the many places of interest around the harbor.

This photo shows the monorail leaving the city center, with Sydney Tower in the background.

Harbor ferries provide a fast and scenic journey from the suburbs to the city.

Sydney captured the world's attention when it hosted the 2000 Summer Olympics. Ships and airplanes with people from around the world arrived in Sydney. With its fascinating blend of ancient and modern culture, it is truly one of the world's greatest cities.

Appendix Fast Facts

	London	New York	Toronto	Sydney
Location	southeastern England, United Kingdom	New York State, United States	Ontario, Canada	New South Wales, Australia
Estimated Population, 2003 (Metropolitan Area)	7 million	9 million	5 million	4 million
Average January Temperature	39°Fahrenheit	33°Fahrenheit	24°Fahrenheit	73°Fahrenheit
Average July Temperature	63°Fahrenheit	74°Fahrenheit	71°Fahrenheit	56°Fahrenheit
Average Annual Rainfall	30 inches	44 inches	32 inches	48 inches
Places to Visit	• British Museum • Buckingham Palace • London Eye • Tower of London • Westminster Abbey	• Central Park • Coney Island • Empire State Building • Metropolitan Museum of Art • Statue of Liberty	• CN Tower • Harbourfront • Ontario Science Centre • Royal Ontario Museum • SkyDome	• Manly Beach • Powerhouse Museum • Sydney Harbour Bridge • Sydney Opera House • Taronga Zoo

Glossary

Aboriginal peoples of or relating to the first peoples of a country

cosmopolitan worldly, belonging to all parts of the world

emigrated left one country or region to settle in another

ethnic relating to races or large groups of people classed according to common traits or customs

exported sent goods from one country to another country for sale and use

financial of or relating to money resources

immigrants people who move to a country to take up permanent residence

imported brought goods in from another country for sale and use

manufacturing the act of making something from raw materials

metropolis the main city of a state, country, or region

metropolitan area an area made up of a large city and its surrounding cities and towns

monorail a railway with a single rail serving as a track

multicultural relating to a mix of several distinct cultures

omnibuses large public buses, or historically, horse-drawn carriages

penal of or relating to punishment

slums parts of a city where many people, especially poor people, live in crowded, run-down conditions

stock exchanges places where stocks and bonds are bought and sold

Index